TRUMP IN HIS OWN WORDS

"I HAVE THE BEST WORDS."
- DONALD TRUMP
APRIL 5, 2017

Compiled by
The Contemporary Policy Institute

authorHOUSE®

AuthorHouse™
1663 Liberty Drive
Bloomington, IN 47403
www.authorhouse.com
Phone: 833-262-8899

Published by AuthorHouse 06/14/2023

ISBN: 979-8-8230-0358-2 (sc)
ISBN: 979-8-8230-0359-9 (e)

Library of Congress Control Number: 2023908148

Print information available on the last page.

This book is printed on acid-free paper.

INTRODUCTION

Whatever may be true about Donald Trump, he has an undeniable genius for commanding the news cycle. Arriving on the political scene just as social media was becoming an accepted platform for public communication, he has supplied supporters and detractors alike with a tsunami of quotes, rants, and tweets, supplemented by quotes and commentary from the flood of "insider" books and articles.

He has tweeted so much about so many topics, that his thoughts can seem ephemeral, destined to be lost in the fog of political spin and short-term memory loss. Quantity on the Trumpian scale can dull the senses and fog the memory.

But it is important to capture and preserve his unique style of public communication. From "I alone can fix it," to "Who knew health care could be so complicated," the Trump corpus of public comments have a unique flavor and individual signature. Few if any of his tweets could be attributed to anyone else. He is never anodyne, never soft, always on the attack, always willing to break established conventions and norms.

This volume is our attempt to preserve a representative sample of Trump's public comments on various topics. Our researchers have waded through thousands of quotes and selected a few hundred which highlight his unique style and flavor. We have arranged them around five specific topics, Women, Health Care, the Environment, Ukraine and NATO, supplemented by a grab bag of miscellaneous comments spread over the entire universe of public and private matters.

Each quote is accompanied by a citation of the source. Where necessary, numbered Notes at the end of each section supply relevant historical context.

Many, both in the media and everyday conversation, have talked and argued endlessly about Trump. This collection is intended to anchor those conversations. Instead of paraphrasing or working from faulty memory, this collection is intended to help us all talk about Trump "In His own Words."

CPI Media is proud to add this volume to the distinguished line of thoughts and quotes from other notable leaders, right between Mao's "Little Black Book," and "The Wit and Wisdom of JFK."

Andy Thorburn
President, CPI Media, Inc.

TRUMP ON WOMEN

"Nobody has more respect for women than I do. Nobody. Nobody has more respect."
October 2016 Presidential Debate

1. "You know, it really doesn't matter what they write as long as you've got a young and beautiful piece of ass. But she's got to be young and beautiful."

   1991 Esquire Interview

2. "I am going to be dating her in 10 years. Can you believe it?"

   1992 (leaked recording about a 10-year-old girl passing by on the escalator)

3. "You have to treat 'em (women) like shit."

   1992 New York magazine

4. "Women are really a lot different than portrayed. They are far worse than men, far more aggressive."

   1997 "The Art of the Comeback"

5. "Don't you think my daughter's hot? She's hot, right?"

   1998 The New York Times via Vox

6. "I have a deal with her. She's just 17 and doing great, Ivanka. And she made me promise or swear to her that I would never date a girl younger than her. So, Howard, as she grows older, the field is getting very limited. To deal with, you know." "The nerve of her, now you can't go out with 16-year-olds." (Stern)

   1997 The Howard Stern Show

7. "You know who's one of the great beauties of the world, according to everybody? And I helped create her. Ivanka. My daughter, Ivanka. She's 6 feet tall, she's got the best

body. She made a lot of money as a model - a tremendous amount."

2003 The Howard Stern Show

8. "All of the women on 'The Apprentice' flirted with me, consciously or unconsciously. That's to be expected."

2004 "The Art of the Comeback"

9. "You never get to the face because the body's so good."

September 2004 The Week

(On Steffi Graf)

10. "What do you think of Lindsay Lohan? (Then 18 years old). There's something there, right? But you have to like freckles. I've seen a close-up of her chest. And a lot of freckles. Are you into freckles?... She's probably deeply troubled, and therefore great in bed. How come the deeply troubled women — deeply, deeply troubled — they're always the best in bed? You don't want to be with 'em for the long term. But for the short term, there's nothing like it."

2004 interview with Howard Stern

11. "I'm automatically attracted to beautiful women — I just start kissing them. It's like a magnet. Just kiss. I don't even wait. When you're a star, they let you do it. You can do anything. Grab 'em by the pussy. You can do anything."

2005 secret video recording, "Access Hollywood"

12. "I like kids. I mean, I won't do anything to take care of them. I'll supply funds and she'll take care of the kids. It's not like I'm gonna be walking the kids down Central Park."

2005 interview with Howard Stern

13. "How do the breasts look?"
(On wife Melania Trump, when asked if he would stay with her if she was disfigured in a car crash.)

April 2005 "The Howard Stern Show"

14. "There's a lot of women out there that demand that the husband act like the wife and you know there's a lot of husbands that listen to that."

2005 radio interview

15. "Can you imagine the parents of Kelli Carpenter (Rosie O'Donnell's first wife) when she said, 'Mom, Dad, I just fell in love with a big, fat pig named Rosie?'"

December 2006 Fox interview
(On Rosie O'Donnell)

16. "I don't think Ivanka would do that, although she does have a very nice figure. I've said if Ivanka weren't my daughter, perhaps I'd be dating her. Isn't that terrible? How terrible? Is that terrible?"

December 2006 "The View" (On Ivanka posing for Playboy Magazine)

17. "She's actually always been very voluptuous. She's tall, she's almost 6 feet tall and she's been, she's an amazing beauty."

2006 "The Howard Stern Show"
(When asked if Ivanka has had breast augmentation)

18. "I've known Jeff for 15 years. Terrific guy. He's a lot of fun to be with. It is even said that he likes beautiful women as much as I do, and many of them are on the younger side. No doubt about it, Jeffrey enjoys his social life."

2008 Vox
(On Jeffrey Epstein)

19. "Sarah Jessica Parker voted 'un-sexiest woman alive' – I agree."

October 2012 Facebook

20. "Unattractive both inside and out. I fully understand why her former husband left her for a man - he made a good decision."

2012 Tweet
(On Arianna Huffington)

21. "I promise not to talk about your massive plastic surgeries that didn't work."

November 2012 Tweet
(On Cher)

22. "26,000 unreported sexual assaults in the military – only 238 convictions. What did these geniuses expect when they put men & women together?"

May 2013 Tweet
(On sexual assaults in the military)

23. "I love her ...upper body."

July 2013 The Daily Beast
(On Halle Berry)

24. "Rosie is crude, rude, obnoxious and dumb – other than that I like her very much."

July 2014 Tweet
(On Rosie O'Donnell)

25. "If Hillary Clinton can't satisfy her husband, what makes her think she can satisfy America?"

April 2015 campaign rally
(On Hillary Clinton)

26. "There was blood coming out of her eyes, blood coming out of her wherever."

August 2015 televised debate moderated by Megyn Kelly
(On being challenged by Megyn Kelly on his many past misogynistic comments)

27. "I don't know how you would define insecurity as it pertains to me."

August 2015 The New York Times interview by Maureen Dowd

28. "One thing I have learned: There is high maintenance. There is low maintenance. I want no maintenance."

2015 The Washington Post, "The Art of the Comeback"

29. "Heidi Klum. Sadly, she's no longer a 10."

August 2015 The New York Times interview

30. "Even a race to Obama, she was gonna beat Obama. I don't know who would be worse, I don't know, how could it be worse? But she was going to beat -- she was favored to win -- and she got schlonged, she lost, I mean she lost."

2015 CNN interview

(On Hillary Clinton)

31. "Look at that face. Would anybody vote for that? Can you imagine that the face of our next president? I mean, she's a woman, and I'm not supposed to say bad things, but really, folks, come on. Are we serious?"

November 2015 campaign rally (source: Mediaite)

(On Carly Fiorina

32. "Hillary Clinton is a major national security risk. Not presidential material!"

January 2016 Tweet

33. "Another radical Islamic attack, this time in Pakistan, targeting Christian women & children. At least 67 dead, 400 injured. I alone can solve."

March 2016 Tweet

34. "The doctor or any other person performing this illegal act upon a woman would be held legally responsible, not the woman."

March 2016 MSNBC Town Hall

(On comments he made that women who have abortions should be punished)

35. "The press is going out of their way to convince people that I do not like or respect women, when they know that it is just the opposite!"

March 2016 Tweet

36. "If she were a man, I don't think she'd get five percent of the vote. The only thing she's got going is the women's card. And the beautiful thing is, women don't like her."

April 2016 news conference at Trump Tower
(On Hillary Clinton)

37. "Pocahontas is at it again. Goofy Elizabeth Warren, one of the least productive US Senators, has a nasty mouth."

June 2016 Tweet

38. "Hillary Clinton is unfit to be president. She has bad judgement, poor leadership skills and a very bad and destructive track record. Change!"

June 2016 Tweet

39. "Hillary Clinton should not be given national security briefings in that she is a loose cannon with extraordinarily bad judgement &instincts."

July 2016 Tweet

40. "She doesn't have the look. She doesn't have the stamina, I said she doesn't have the stamina, and I don't believe she does have the stamina."

September 2016 Tweet
(On Hillary Clinton)

41. "I really do believe that Clinton doesn't look the part. I just don't believe she has a presidential look, and you need a presidential look."

September 2016 interview on ABC news with David Muir

42. "Believe me, she would not be my first choice, that I can tell you. Man, you don't know, that would not be my first choice."

October 2016 rally

On Jessica Leeds (accusing Trump of sexually molesting her on a plane several years earlier)

43. "These events never, ever happened, and the people that said them, meekly, fully understand. You take a look at these people, you study these people, and you'll understand also."

October 2016 speech in Florida

(On 28 women coming forward accusing Trump of assault)

44. "I would like to think she would find another career or find another company if that was the case."

2016 USA Today

(On what he would like Ivanka to do if she was ever harassed at work)

45. "So what do we got to pay for this, $150 thousand?"

2016 secret audiotape recording of Trump and Cohen

(Discussing with Michael Cohen payment to former Playboy model Karen McDougal)

46. "The media has deceived the public by putting women front and center with made-up stories and lies and got caught."

October 2016 Tweet

47. "Can you believe I lost large numbers of women voters based on made up events THAT NEVER HAPPENED. Media rigging election!"

October 2016 Tweet

48. "Can't believe these totally phoney stories, 100% made up by women (many already proven false) and pushed big time by press!"

October 2016 Tweet

49. "I have tremendous respect for women and the many roles they serve that are vital to the fabric of our society and our economy."

March 2017 Tweet

50. "I heard poorly rated_@Morning_Joe speaks badly of me (don't watch anymore). Then how come low I.Q. Crazy Mika, along with Psycho Joe, came to Mar-a-Lago 3 nights in a row around New Year's Eve, and insisted on joining me. She was bleeding badly from a face-lift. I said no!"

2017 Tweet
(On Mika Brzezinski)

51. "You're in such good shape. She's in such good physical shape. Beautiful,"

July 2017 CNN
(To French First Lady Brigitte Macron)

52. "Someone who would come to my office 'begging' for campaign contributions not so long ago (and would do anything for them)."

December 2017 Tweet
(On Democratic Sen. Kirsten Gillibrand)

53. "Does she have a good body? No. Does she have a fat ass? Absolutely."

February 2018 "Howard Stern Show"
(On Kim Kardashian)

54. "My daughter, Ivanka, just arrived in South Korea. We cannot have a better, or smarter, person representing our country."

February 2018 Tweet

55. "No."
Responding to question if he knew about $130,000 payment by his attorney Michael Cohen to Stormy Daniels."You'll

have to ask Michael Cohen. Michael is my attorney, and you'll have to ask Michael Cohen."

April 2018 reply to Intelligencer reporter
(When asked if he knew why Cohen paid her)

56. "An extraordinarily low IQ person."

June 2018 Tweet
(On Democratic Rep. Maxine Waters)

57. "AOC is a Whack Job!"

October 2019 Tweet
(On Democratic Rep. Alexandria Ocasio-Cortez)

58. "When you give a crazed, crying lowlife a break, and give her a job at the White House, I guess it didn't work out. Good work by General Kelly for quickly firing that dog!"

August 2018 Tweet
(On Omarosa Manigault Newman)

59. "You've got to deny, deny, deny and push back on these women. If you admit to anything and any culpability, then you're dead. ... You've got to be strong. You've got to be aggressive. You've got to push back hard. You've got to deny anything that's said about you. Never admit."

September 2018 "Fear: Trump in the White House" by Bob Woodward

60. "Great, now I can go after Horseface (Stormy Daniels) and her 3rd rate lawyer in the Great State of Texas."

October 2018 Tweet

61. "I'll say it with great respect: Number one, she's not my type. Number two, it never happened,"

June 2019 The Hill
(On advice-columnist E. Jean Carroll suing Trump for defamation)

62. "Because Nancy's teeth were falling out of her mouth, and she didn't have time to think!"

December 2019
(On Nancy Pelosi)

63. "She will go down as perhaps the least successful Speaker in U.S. History."

January 2020 Tweet
(On Nancy Pelosi)

64. "This is not even a smart person, other than she's got a good line of stuff. I mean, she goes out and she yaps."

August 2020 Fox Business Network
(On Democratic Rep. Alexandria Ocasio-Cortez)

65. "I have done more for WOMEN than just about any President in HISTORY!"

August 2020 Tweet

66. "She's a slob. How does she even get on television? If I were running 'The View,' I'd fire Rosie. I'd look her right in that fat, ugly face of hers and say, 'Rosie, you're fired.'"

October 2020 Tweet

67. "This monster that was on stage with Mike Pence, who destroyed her last night, by the way. I thought that wasn't even a contest last night. She was terrible. I don't think you could get worse. And totally unlikeable."

October 2020 campaign event NPR interview
(On Kamala Harris)

NOTES

Notes are numbered to correspond with quotes.

5. **On daughter Ivanka:** Trump was overheard making this comment to Ms. Lee of the Miss Teen USA Pageant.

6. **Howard Stern** Is an American radio and TV personality. He was one of the original "shock jocks" known for his provocative interviews of celebrities since 1975. He is known for asking personal, often outrageous questions and making inappropriate comments.

8. "**The Apprentice"** was a reality game show which aired from January 2004 to 2017. Trump hosted the first 14 seasons.

9. **Steffi Graf** is a German former professional tennis player. She was ranked world No. 1 for a record 377 weeks and won 22 major singles titles, third-most of all-time.

10. **Lindsay Lohan** is an actress, starring notably in "Mean Girls," born in New York in July 1986.

11. "**Access Hollywood"** is a weekday entertainment TV show that premiered in 1996. The show focuses on the "hottest" stories in Hollywood. The quote comes from a recorded conversation between Trump and host Billy Bush regarding a guest they are about to meet.

15. **Rosie O'Donnell** is an American comedian, television producer, actress, author, and television personality.

16. "**The View"** is a daytime panel talk show on ABC hosted exclusively by women. First released in 1997, topics covered by the panel usually involve celebrity gossip and political events.

18. **Jeffrey Epstein** (Jeffrey Edward Epstein) was an American convicted sex offender and former financier. Epstein was born January 1953 in New York City and died August 10, 2019, by suicide at the Metropolitan Correctional Center in New York. Epstein had a previous conviction in Florida for procuring a child for prostitution and for soliciting a prostitute. A socialite with many famous and influential contacts, he allegedly provided underage girls for sex to a number of

friends in his social circle. A number of conspiracy theories surrounding the manner of his death remain current.

19. **Sarah Jessica Parker** is an American actress and television producer. She is the recipient of six Golden Globe Awards and two Primetime Emmy Awards. Time Magazine named her one of the 100 most influential people in the world in 2022.

20. **Arianna Huffington** is a Greek American author, syndicated columnist and businesswoman. She is a co-founder of The Huffington Post and founder / CEO of Thrive Global.

21. **Cher** is an American singer, actress and television personality. Often referred to as the Goddess of Pop, she began her career with Sonny Bono in the early 1960s as Sonny and Cher.

23. **Halle Berr**y is an Oscar-winning American actress. She has co-starred in a James Bond movie, played comic book characters, and starred in over 50 movies.

25. **Hillary Clinton** is a former first lady of the United States and New York senator who ran for president in 2008 but lost to Barack Obama in the primaries. She served in the Obama administration as secretary of state from 2009 to 2013.

26. **Megyn Kelly** is an American journalist, attorney, political commentator, talk show host, and television news anchor. Kelly was one of the moderators of one of the 2015 presidential debates.

27. **Maureen Dowd** is an American columnist for The New York Times. She writes about American politics, popular culture, and international affairs. She won a Pulitzer Prize in 1999 for Distinguished Commentary. Dowd frequently mocked Trump in her articles and commentary including a detailed piece entitled “All the President’s Insecurities.”

29. **Heidi Klum** is a German and American model, television host, producer, and business person. She appeared on the cover of the Sports Illustrated swimsuit Issue in 1998 and is considered one of the original supermodels.

30. **Hillary Clinton** is a former U.S. senator, diplomat and lawyer who was U.S. secretary of state from 2009 to 2013 in the Obama administration and a presidential candidate in the 2016 election which she lost to Donald Trump. "Shlonged" derives from the Yiddish "'shlong" or slang for penis.

31. **Carly Fiorina** is an American businesswoman and politician. Known primarily for her tenure as CEO of Hewlett-Packard from 1999 to 2005. Fiorina was the first woman to lead a Fortune Top 20 company. She was a Republican nominee for U.S. Senate in California in 2010 and was a presidential candidate in 2016.

32. **Hillary Clinton security risk:** Hillary Clinton is the former U.S. first lady, senator, and secretary of state.

33. **Islamic insurgent attack:** Trump continued to ramp up the rhetoric on immigration and anti-Muslim sentiment in the run up to the election.

34. **Abortion:** Trump has had at least five clearly divergent and often contradictory views on abortion over the years:
    1) April 1989: Trump sponsored a dinner to honor Robin Chandler Duke, former president of NARAL (National Association for the Repeal of Abortion Laws).
    2) October 1999: In an interview with Tim Russert of NBC, "I'm very pro-choice."
    3) 2011 at the Conservative Political Action Conference: "I am pro-life and against gun control."
    4) June 2015 interview with Jake Tapper: 'Let me ask you about some social issues, I know you're against abortion.'"Right, I'm pro-choice."

5) March 2016 interview with Chris Matthews, "Women who receive abortions should face punishment." (Source for all above is Washington Post)

36. **2016 presidential election:** Hillary Clinton easily won the popular vote, beating Trump by 2.9 million votes.

37. **Pocahontas:** Trump gave the nickname "Pocahontas" to Sen. Elizabeth Warren during the 2016 election campaign, after her previous claims of having Native American heritage. Trump accused Warren of a dishonest ploy to claim minority status.

40. **Presidential look:** One of many Trump's criticisms of Hillary Clinton. At the time, a CNN / Opinion Research Corporation poll found that among all registered female voters 62% preferred Clinton's temperament over Trump's.

42. **Jessica Leeds** is a former businesswoman who accused Trump of assault aboard a plane in the early 1980s. She went public with her accusations during the 2016 election, which served as a catalyst for 20-plus women who then went public with their sexual misconduct revelations and accusations against Trump.

45. **Karen McDougal** is a former Playboy model who claims to have had an affair with Trump two years after he had married Melania Trump. McDougal memorialized the affair in a document in November 2016, four days before the election. The Wall Street Journal published a story that American Media, parent company of the National Enquirer, had paid $150,000 for the exclusive rights to the story and then never ran it.

48. **Sexual misconduct accusations:** 20-plus women have accused Trump of sexual misconduct and/or assault between 1980 and 2016 accusations include rape, groping, forced kissing, and digital penetration.

36. **Stormy Daniels payment:** The conversation between Trump and his lawyer Michael Cohen was recorded and was broadcast by CNN. It concerns a payment to adult film star Stormy Daniels to stop her going public with details of the affair she had with Trump, which he denies.

44. **Maxine Waters** is an American politician serving as the U.S. representative for California's 43rd Congressional District, which she has served since 1991.

45. **Omarosa Manigault Newman**, also known as Omarosa, is an American reality television show participant ("The Apprentice"), writer, and former political aide to former President Donald Trump.

50. **Mika Brzezinski** is an American journalist, talk show host, liberal political commentator, and author who currently co-hosts MSNBC's show "Morning Joe."

51. **Brigitte Macron** is the wife of French President Emmanuel Macron. At the time of this quote, she was 64.

52. **Kirsten Gillibrand** is an American lawyer and Democratic politician serving as United States Senator from New York since 2009. She served as a member of the U.S. House of Representatives from 2007 to 2009.

54. **Ivanka Trump in South Korea:** Ivanka attended the closing ceremonies of the Olympic Games in Seoul in February 2018. While the visit was seen as a charm offensive, it was also to emphasise the U.S. stance of maintaining maximum pressure on North Korea, contrary to the preferred South Korean strategy of establishing dialogue.

55. **Stormy Daniels** (Stephanie Gregory Clifford) is an American adult film actress, director, and former stripper. She allegedly had a sexual encounter with Trump when she was 27 and he was 60, which Trump has denied. However,

he did pay her $130,000 to keep quiet about the alleged encounter.

56. **Maxine Waters** is an American Democratic politician, born in 1938, who has represented California's 43rd Congressional District since 1991.

57. **Alexandria Ocasio-Cortez**, also known as AOC, is an American politician and activist. She has served as the U.S. representative for New York's 14th Congressional District since 2019.

59. "**Deny, deny, deny":** Bob Woodward is the renowned journalist who broke the Watergate story along with his colleague Carl Bernstein, effectively ending the presidency of Richard Nixon.

60. **Stormy Daniels defamation case**: After a judge in Los Angeles dismissed a defamation case against Trump by Stormy Daniels, Trump intimated he would pursue her in Texas. Following appeals by Daniels, courts eventually ruled in 2020 that the verdict should stand and that she was liable for over $300,000 in legal fees.

61. **E. Jean Carroll:** Elizabeth Jean Carroll is an American journalist, author, and advice columnist. Her "Ask E. Jean" column appeared in Elle magazine from 1993 through 2019, becoming one of the longest-running advice columns in American publishing. In a still running lawsuit, she claimed Trump raped her in a department store in the 1990s.

62. **Tweet in reference to Nancy Pelosi** press conference answering the question why she didn't make "bribery" a central part of the articles of impeachment. Pelosi had specifically accused Trump of bribery for threatening to withhold military aid in exchange for information on a political rival.

63. **Nancy Pelosi** announced her retirement as Speaker of the House in November 2022 after more than two decades of Democratic leadership. She was the nation's first female U.S. House speaker and was lauded by both political sides as an example of how to navigate the challenges of political life. Her ability to unite her caucus to pass key legislation in tumultuous times, along with her long tenure, has confirmed her place as the most powerful woman in politics to date.

66. **Rosie O'Donnell:** Trump's seeming never-ending dislike of Rosie O'Donnell on full display.

67. **Vice Presidential debate:** Referring to the vice presidential candidates debate that took place on October 8, 2020, between Mike Pence and Kamala Harris.

VIDEO COMPILATION of Trump making outrageous comments about various women
https://www.youtube.com/watch?v=-55hPvPnTOU

VIDEO COMPILATION II More outrageous Trump quotes about women
https://www.youtube.com/watch?v=H6PPB9N8Ax8

VIDEO and AUDIO of **"Grab them by the pussy."**
https://www.youtube.com/watch?v=fYqKx1GuZGg

VIDEO "ACCESS HOLLYWOOD" TAPE extended version
https://www.youtube.com/watch?v=WhsSzIS84ks

TRUMP ON THE ENVIRONMENT

"I'm an environmentalist. A lot of people don't understand that. I think I know more about the environment than most people."
October 2020 Tweet

1. "The concept of global warming was created by and for the Chinese in order to make U.S. manufacturing non-competitive."

   November 2012 Tweet

2. "The Chinese are illegally dumping bird-killing wind turbines on our shores. Only one of many grievances – we should act."

   July 2012 Tweet

3. "It's Friday. How many bald eagles did wind turbines kill today? They are an environmental & aesthetic disaster."

   August 2012 Tweet

4. "Windmills are a bigger safety hazard than either coal or oil. A 34% higher mortality rate than coal alone. Outrageous!"

   November 2012 Tweet

5. "Fracking poses ZERO health risks."

   May 2013 Tweet

6. "Ice storm rolls from Texas to Tennessee -- I'm in Los Angeles and it's freezing. Global warming is a total, and very expensive, hoax!"

   December 2013 Tweet

7. "Obama's coal regulations will destroy the coal industry, put Americans out of work, raise electricity prices & lead to blackouts."

   September 2013 Tweet

8. "Fact: without Texas and states reaping the fracking boom, Obama's job record would go from bad to worse!"

August 2013 Tweet

9. "The con artists changed the name from GLOBAL WARMING to CLIMATE CHANGE when GLOBAL WARMING was no longer working, and credibility was lost!"

December 2013 Tweet

10. "Upstate New York is suffering with record unemployment. Fracking is the answer. Frack now and frack fast!"

August 2013 Tweet

11. "Give me clean, beautiful, and healthy air -- not the same old climate change (global warming) bullshit! I am tired of hearing this nonsense."

January 2014 Tweet

12. "Do you believe this one -- Secretary of State John Kerry just stated that the most dangerous weapon of all today is climate change. Laughable."

February 2014 Tweet

13. "It's not climate change, it's global warming. Don't let the dollar sucking wise guys change names midstream because the first name didn't work."

February 2014 Tweet

14. "Obama's wind turbines kill 13-39 million birds and bats every year!"

May 2014 Tweet

15. "It's late in July and it is really cold outside in New York. Where the hell is GLOBAL WARMING??? We need some fast! It's now CLIMATE CHANGE."

July 2014 Tweet

16. "President Obama was terrible on 60 Minutes tonight. He said CLIMATE CHANGE is the most important thing, not all of the current disasters!"

    October 2015 Tweet

17. "Why can't we use nuclear weapons?"

    August 2016 Trump quizzes foreign policy advisers (recorded during meeting)

18. "Trump signs bill undoing Obama coal mining rule."

    February 2017 Tweet

19. "We're going to have clean coal, really clean coal."

    March 2017 executive order launch

20. "Among the lowest temperatures EVER in much of the United States. Ice caps at record size. Changed name from GLOBAL WARMING to CLIMATE CHANGE."

    February 2017 Tweet

21. "The energy we produce in our country is cleaner than our foreign competitors."

    2017 source: Friends of the Earth

22. "It's freezing and snowing in New York -- we need global warming!"

    December 29, 2017 Tweet

23. "You wanna see a bird cemetery? Go under a windmill sometime. It's the saddest – you've got every type of bird."

    2017 source: Friends of the Earth

24. "It is finally happening for our great clean coal miners!"

    November 2017 Tweet

25. "I'm not a believer in man-made global warming. It could be warming, and it's going to start to cool at some point. And

you know, in the early, in the 1920s, people talked about global cooling. ... They thought the Earth was cooling."

2017 source: Manufacturing Business Technology publication

26. "There is cooling, and there's heating. I mean, look, it used to not be climate change, it used to be global warming. That wasn't working too well because it was getting too cold all over the place."

January 28, 2018 Piers Morgan interview

27. "The ice caps were going to melt; they were going to be gone by now. But now they're setting records. They're at record level."

January 2018 Piers Morgan interview

28. "America is blessed with extraordinary energy abundance, including more than 250 years' worth of beautiful clean coal. We have ended the war on coal and will continue to work to promote American energy dominance!"

May 2018 Tweet

29. "When I came here originally, West Virginia, frankly, was down and out. It was not doing exactly well. One of the last. Do you know that a few months ago, it hit where West Virginia is, on a per capita basis, one of the most successful GDP states in our union?"

2018 campaign rally

30. "Under the green new deal, they don't like clean, beautiful natural gas. The green new deal don't know what they like."

July 2018

31. "I'm not denying climate change. But it could very well go back. You know, we're talking about over a million of years. They say that we had hurricanes that were far worse than what we just had with Michael."

October 2018 "60 Minutes"

32. "We love clean, beautiful West Virginia coal. We love it. And you know that's indestructible stuff. In times of war, in times of conflict, you can blow up those windmills. They fall down really quick. You can blow up those pipelines. They go like this and you're not going to fix them too fast. You can do a lot of things to those solar panels. But you know what you can't hurt? Coal."

    2018 campaign rally

33. "I want clean air. I want crystal clean water. And we've got it. We've got the cleanest country on the planet right now. There's nobody cleaner than us."

    2018 Tweet

34. "The badly flawed Paris Climate Agreement protects the polluters, hurts Americans, and costs a fortune. NOT ON MY WATCH! I want crystal clean water and the cleanest and the purest air on the planet – we've now got that!"

    September 2019 Tweet

35. "South Carolina, North Carolina, Georgia, and Alabama will most likely be hit (much) harder than anticipated by the storm."

    September 2019 Tweet

36. "Why don't we nuke them? We drop a bomb inside the eye of the hurricane, and it disrupts it. Why can't we do that?"

    2019 hurricane briefing at the White House

37. "Climate change is very important to me. I've done many environmental impact statements in my life, and I believe very strongly in very, very crystal-clear clean water and clean air."

    December 2019 conversation with reporters

38. "They take a shower and water comes dripping out, just dripping out, very quietly dripping out. People are flushing toilets 10 times, 15 times, as opposed to once."

    December 2019 campaign rally in Milwaukee

39. "I'm an environmentalist. A lot of people don't understand that. I think I know more about the environment than most people."

October 2020 Tweet

41. "I heard from someone that the ocean is going to rise one eighth of an inch. No one is really worried about that, just means we are going to have more beachfront property."

July 9, 2022 Campaign rally, Anchorage Alaska

42. "Department of Environmental Protection: We are going to get rid of it in almost every form. We're going to have little tidbits left. But we're going to take a tremendous amount out."

March 16, 2016 Republican Primary Debate

NOTES

Notes are numbered to correspond to quotes.

4. Studies conducted by environmental nonprofit ecoRI (ecoRhode Island News) notes wind facilities are responsible for between 0.3 and 0.4 fatalities per gigawatt-hour of electricity, compared to fossil fuel power plants which are responsible for 5.2 fatalities per gigawatt-hour.
   Source: https://ecori.org/2018-1-22-stop-the-spin-wind-turbines-kill-less-birds-than-fossil-fuels/#:~:text=It%20concluded%20 that%20wind%20facilities,5.2%20 fatalities%20 per%20 gigawatt%2d Hour.

5. Hydraulic fracturing (fracking) technology consists of high-pressure fluid injections to shatter rock formations and extract natural gas. It is blamed for leaking millions of tons of methane into the atmosphere. Fracking also uses large amounts of water which can be easily contaminated and affect local groundwater.
   Source: https://www.investopedia.com/ask/answers/011915/what-are-effects-fracking-environment.asp

6. "Observations throughout the world make it clear that climate change is occurring, and rigorous scientific research demonstrates that the greenhouse gases emitted by human activities are the primary driver."
   Source: NASA https://climate.nasa.gov/scientific-consensus/

7. President Barack Obama announced new EPA regulations in June 2014 to reduce carbon pollution from coal plants by 30%. By the time these regulations came into effect, demand for U.S. coal had plummeted. A 2016 report by the Center on Global Energy Policy identified the market forces responsible for the decline in U.S. coal including replacement by natural gas (fracking) and renewable energy. New regulations contributed to only a 3-5% drop in coal market share.
   Source: https://www.worldenergy.org/assets/images/imported/2016/10/World-Energy-Resources-Full-report-2016.10.03.pdf

9. Global warming refers to global temperatures rising over time, primarily due to increasing greenhouse gases in the atmosphere. Climate change refers to changes in weather patterns and the measures of climate over a long period of time – including precipitation, temperature, and wind patterns.

10. Most employment statistics are produced by the industry-funded American Petroleum Institute (API) which claims domestic fracking creates between 2.5 and 11 million jobs. Independent, non-industry funded reports put the actual number at under 500,000 or 0.4% of all employment. Since 2014, oil and gas employment has fallen 33% while production has increased 32%.
    Source: Food & Water Watch https://inthesetimes.com/article/fossil-fuel-fracking-climate-action-labor-union-jobs

14. Three major U.S. studies (2022) estimate wind turbine bird deaths at 100,000 to 450,000 a year. Birds killed by collisions with buildings are recorded at 1 billion per year in the U.S. Cats kill 1 to 4 billion birds in the U.S. per year.

18. The Tweet refers to the ending of Obama era environmental regulations, particularly those pertaining to protecting waterways from coal pollution. The Trump administration claimed the rules cost jobs but according to virtually every independent source, the regulations counted for a very minor part of decreasing employment in the coal industry. Fracking, lower demand, renewables and lower exports were the real cause.
    Source: https://www.vox.com/energy-and-environment/2017/4/28/15465348/obama-trump-regulations-coal

19. The executive order was issued to loosen regulatory controls of every federal agency on the fossil fuel industry. Trump instructed all departments to identify and target for eliminate any rules that would restrict energy production. He also put controls in place that would make it much more difficult to reinstate such controls in the future.
    Source: https://insideclimatenews.org/news/28032017/trump-exe-cutive-order-climate-change-paris-climate-agreement-clean-power-plan-pruitt/

20. There are hundreds of tweets from Trump starting around 2011 that sow confusion between weather events and global warming, suggesting they are the same. We chose just one. For a detailed list, check:
    https://www.vox.com/policy-and-politics/2017/6/1/15726472/trump-tweets-global-warming-paris-mate-agreement

21. Presumably this is a reference to the fact the U.S. was producing 18% of the nation's power from renewables at the time of this comment. It omits that many competitors around the world produce more power from renewables than the U.S. and burn less fossil fuel.

23. Another claim that wind turbines are responsible for bird deaths. Mortality rates for birds by wind turbines are a fraction of those for birds killed by buildings and cats. 0.03% of bird deaths are due to wind turbines. Notably, Britain's

RSPB (Royal Society for the Protection of Birds) supports wind turbines.

24. Trump claims to have ended the "War on coal." In fact, more closures and job losses occurred.

25. More than 99.9% of peer-reviewed scientific papers agree that climate change is mainly caused by humans, according to a new survey of 88,125 climate-related studies. **Cornell University** https://news.cornell.edu/stories/2021/10/more-999-studies-agree-humans-caused-climate-change

32. "Every year, climatic disasters cause human suffering as well as large economic and ecological damage. Over the past decade, direct damages of such disasters are estimated to add up to around US $1.3 trillion (or around 0.2% of world GDP on average, per year)." **International Monetary Fund** https://www.imf.org/en/Topics/climate-change/climate-and-the-economy#:~:text=Every%20year%2C%20climatic%20disasters%20cause,on%20average%2C%20per%20year).in the coal sector under his tenure than in Obama's second term. Source: https://www.eenews.net/articles/more-coal-has-retired-under- trump-than-in-obamas-2nd-term/

26. There is a myth among climate change deniers that earth's cooling and warming trends are natural phenomena not caused by humans. They omit the fact that the speed and degree of high temperature changes are completely without parallel. Seventeen of the last 18 record-setting years occurred since 2001. The rapid warming corresponds with increasing levels of carbon dioxide. https://apnews.com/article/north-america-donald-trump-ap-top-news-piers-morgan-oceans-4a89b1accf89460097fb52fb7e307f90

27. Ice caps in Greenland and Antarctica are losing staggering amounts of ice per year. The ice thickness is now less than

50% of what it was 40 years ago, according to the National Snow and Ice Data Center.

28. "Climate change is coal's most serious, long-term, global impact. Chemically, coal is mostly carbon, which, when burned, reacts with oxygen in the air to produce carbon dioxide, a heat-trapping gas. When released into the atmosphere, carbon dioxide works like a blanket, warming the earth above normal limits." Union of Concerned Citizens https://www.ucsusa.org/resources/coal-power-impacts

29. At the time of this writing, West Virginia was the fifth-poorest state and had the lowest level of higher education in the country. It ranked 47th in healthcare, 45th in education, 50th in infrastructure and 48th in overall economy. https://www.usnews.com/news/best-states/west-virginia

30. The Green New Deal's stated aims are well established, including switching the U.S. economy to renewable energy within the next 10 years. Natural gas is not acceptable because it is a fossil fuel emitting significant amounts of greenhouse gases. The production process creates large amounts of methane which can easily leak into the atmosphere, further warming the planet.

34. The U.S. is ranked 27th out of 180 for environmental performance as reviewed by Yale, Columbia, and the World Economic Forum.

35. The Paris Accord is a non-binding voluntary agreement allowing each participant to set its own targets. There are no membership cost implications to the American public.

36. The Tweet was a warning about imminent Hurricane Dorian and its impact on several states including Alabama which turned out to be erroneous. Trump was quickly corrected by Birmingham National Weather Service. On the next official briefing, it appeared someone had drawn an additional loop

on the map with a Sharpie marker. The doctored map now looked as though Trump had been right about Alabama. The sequence of events became known as Sharpiegate. Source: https://www.vox.com/policy-and-politics/2019/9/6/20851971/trump-hurricane-dorian-alabama-sharpie-cnn-media

37. **Hurricane bombing:** While Trump later denied having said this, several people at the meeting corroborated Axiom's story.

41. National Oceanic and Atmospheric Administration predicts sea-level rise by 10-12 inches along the U.S. Coast by 2050.

42. "The oil and gas industry is not only at the table in the Trump administration, it owns the table and chairs, and is hosting the party. Trump originally appointed ExxonMobil Chief Executive Rex Tillerson as Secretary of State, meaning that a lifelong fossil fuels advocate was representing the U.S. in climate discussions with foreign leaders around the world." Environmental Integrity Project: https://docs.google.com/document/d/1GSWYrVmK47EUYPxNMNOrRQ8bIFlGzsMM/edit

TRUMP ON PUTIN, UKRAINE, AND NATO

"Putin is a nicer person than I am."

1. "Do you think Putin will be going to the Miss Universe pageant in November in Moscow – if so, will he become my new best friend?"

   June 18, 2013 Tweet

2. "So, we've invited President Putin, that'll be interesting. I know he'd like to go."

   September 2013 "Fox and Friends"

3. "Putin has done a really great job outsmarting our country."

October 2013 Larry King on Ora TV

4. "I do have a relationship (*with Putin*) and I can tell you that he's very interested in what we're doing here today. He's probably very interested in what you and I are saying today, and I'm sure he's going to be seeing it in some form, but I do have a relationship with him, and I think it's very interesting to see what's happened."

November 2013 MSNBC

5. "When I went to Russia with the Miss Universe pageant, he (*Putin*) contacted me and was so nice. I mean, the Russian people were so fantastic to us. I'll just say this, they are doing – they're outsmarting us at many turns, as we all understand."

February 2014 "Fox and Friends"

6. "We just left Moscow. He (*Putin*) could not have been nicer. He was so nice and so everything. But you have to give him credit that what he's doing for that country in terms of their world prestige is very strong."

April 2014 Fox Business News

7. "Well, he's done an amazing job of taking the mantle. And he's taken it away from the president (*Obama*), and you look at what he's doing. And so smart. When you see the riots in a country because they're hurting the Russians, OK, 'We'll go and take it over.' And he really goes step by step, and you have to give him a lot of credit."

April 2014 Fox Business News

(On the Russian invasion of the Crimea)

8. "Putin has shown the world what happens when America has weak leaders. Peace Through Strength!"

April 28, 2014, Tweet

9. "Putin is absolutely having a great time. Russia is like, I mean they're really hot stuff."

April 2014 New Hampshire event

10. "I own Miss Universe, I was in Russia, I was in Moscow recently and I spoke, indirectly and directly, with President Putin, who could not have been nicer, and we had a tremendous success."

May 2014 National Press Club

11. "You know I had the Miss Universe contest over in Moscow recently ... Putin treated us unbelievably well. At that time that Putin said, 'They have killings in the streets. Look at what's going on in Chicago and different places. They have all of this turmoil, all of the things that are happening in there.'"

June 20, 2014 The American Spectator

12. "I think I became much richer because I can understand people and read people and Putin is not finished. Putin has got a long way to go."

July 2014 WTOP radio

13. "I think I get along with him (*Putin*) fine. I think he would be absolutely fine. He would never keep somebody like Snowden in Russia. He hates Obama. He doesn't respect Obama. Obama doesn't like him either. But he has no respect for Obama. Has a hatred for Obama. And Snowden is living the life. Look if that – if I'm president, Putin says, hey, boom, you're gone. I guarantee you this."

July 2015 CNN interview with Anderson Cooper

14. "Putin knows that Obama is a danger to the world. Putin will respect President Trump. True!"

July 2015 re-Tweet

15. "Putin hates us. He hates Obama. He doesn't hate us. I think he'd like me. I'd get along great with him, I think. If you want to know the truth."

August 29, 2015 Fox News

16. "I think I'd get along well with Putin. I know many of the people. I had a major event there two years ago in Moscow, as you know. It was a tremendous success. An amazing success. I think I'd get along well with Putin."

August 2015

17. "Putin is a nicer person than I am."

September 2015 to reporters at Trump Tower

18. "I will tell you that I think in terms of leadership, he (*Putin*) is getting an 'A,' and our president is not doing so well. They did not look good together."

September 29, 2015 Bill O'Reilly, Fox News

19. "I think the biggest thing we have is that we were on '60 Minutes' together and we had fantastic ratings. One of your best-rated shows in a long time. So that was good, right? So, we were stablemates."

October 2015 CBS "Face the Nation"

20. "I've always had a good instinct about Putin. I just feel that that's a guy – and I can analyse people and you're not always right, and it could be that I won't like him. But I've always had a good feeling about him from the standpoint."

December 21, 2015 Iowa radio host Simon Conway

21. "He's (*Putin*) running his country and at least he's a leader, unlike what we have in this country. I think our country does plenty of killing also, Joe *(program host*), so you know. There's a lot of stupidity going on in the world right now, a lot of killing going on, a lot of stupidity."

December 2015 MSNBC "Morning Joe"

22. "Have they found him guilty [of the murder of Alexander Litvinenko]? I don't think they've found him guilty. If he did it, fine. But I don't know that he did it. You know, people are saying they think it was him, it might have been him, it could have been him. In all fairness to Putin – I don't know. You know, and I'm not saying this because he says, 'Trump is brilliant and leading everybody' – the fact is that, you know, he hasn't been convicted of anything."

    January 26, 2016 CNN interview

23. "I have no relationship with him [Putin] other than he called me a genius, he said, 'Donald Trump is a genius and he is going to be the leader of the party and he's going to be the leader of the world' or something."

    February 2016 at campaign rally

24. "Putin said good things about me. He said, 'He's a leader and there's no question about it, he's a genius.' So, they all said, the media, they said – you saw it on the debate – they said, 'You admire President Putin.' I said, I don't admire him. I said he was a strong leader, which he is. I mean, he might be bad, he might be good. But he's a strong leader."

    March 2016 rally

25. "Yes, because it's costing us too much money. And frankly they have to put up more money."

    March 21, 2016 CNN interview with Wolf Blitzer

26. "They're [*NATO*] not paying their fair share. That means we are protecting them, giving them military protection and other things, and they're ripping off the United States. And you know what we do? Nothing. Either they have to pay up for past deficiencies or they have to get out. And if it breaks up NATO, it breaks up NATO."

    April 2, 2016 Racine, Wisconsin campaign stop

27. "We're going to have a great relationship with Putin and Russia."

April 2016 victory rally

28. "I said here's the problem with NATO: It's obsolete. Big statement to make when you don't know that much about it, but I learn quickly."

April 2, 2016 in Wausau, Wisconsin

29. "He's not going into Ukraine, OK, just so you understand. You can mark it down. You can put it down."

July 2016 news conference (source: ABC News)

30. "I would treat Vladimir Putin firmly, but there's nothing I can think of that I'd rather do than have Russia friendly, as opposed to the way they are right now."

July 27, 2016 news conference

31. "But you know, the people of Crimea, from what I've heard, would rather be with Russia than where they were. And you have to look at that, also."

July 31, 2016 interview with George Stephanopoulos

32. "Yes. Yes, [I met Putin] a long time ago. We got along great, by the way."

October 2016

33. " Russia, if you're listening, I hope you're able to find the missing 30,000 emails that are missing.

July 27, 2016 CSPAN

34. "Only if they fulfil their obligations to us."

July 2017 interview with the New York Times

(On assisting NATO allies)

35. "I never met Putin. I don't know who Putin is. He said one nice thing about me. He said I'm a genius. I said thank you

very much to the newspaper and that was the end of it. I never met Putin."

July 27, 2017 news conference

36. "NATO is as bad as NAFTA, it's much too costly for us."

June 28, 2018, to G7 leaders, a day before Brussels summit

37. "Defense spending for NATO members was going down for close to 20 years. If you look at a chart, it was like a rollercoaster down, nothing up. And that was going on for a long time."

2019 NATO summit

38. "I knew that he always wanted Ukraine. I used to talk to him about it. I said, 'You can't do it. You're not going to do it.' But I could see that he wanted it."

February 23, 2022 Politico

39. "Here's a guy who's very savvy, I know him very well. Very, very well."

February 2022 radio interview
(On Putin)

40. On Putin's presidential decree recognizing Ukrainian territory as "independent":
"I went in yesterday and there was a television screen, and I said, 'This is genius.' Putin declares a big portion of ... Ukraine. Putin declares it as independent. Oh, that's wonderful. So, Putin is now saying, 'It's independent,' a large section of Ukraine. I said, 'How smart is that?' And he's gonna go in and be a peacekeeper. That's the strongest peace force. We could use that on our southern border. There were more army tanks than I've ever seen. They're gonna keep peace all right."

February 2022 radio interview

41. "They say, 'Trump said Putin's smart.' I mean, he's taking over a country for two dollars of sanctions. I'd say that's

pretty smart. He's taking over a country – really a vast, vast location, a great piece of land with a lot of people, and just walking right in."

February 23, 2022 fundraiser at Mar-a-Lago (recorded)

42. "Putin's invasion of Ukraine ... is genius, Oh, that's wonderful. You gotta say, that's pretty savvy and you know what the response was from Biden? There was no response. They didn't have one for that. No, it's very sad. Very sad."

February 23, 2022, ABC News

43. "The Russian attack on Ukraine is appalling, an outrage and an atrocity that should have never been allowed to occur. We are praying for the proud people of Ukraine. God bless them all."

February 28, 2022 Orlando, Florida

44. "I would do things [about the invasion] but the last thing I would want to do is say it right now."

February 28, 2022 Fox News

45. "By the way, this never would have happened with us."

February 2022 NPR interview

46. "I hope everyone is able to remember that it was me, as president of the United States, that got delinquent NATO members to start paying their dues, which amounted to hundreds of billions of dollars. There would be no NATO if I didn't act strongly and swiftly."

February 28, 2022 Rolling Stone magazine

NOTES

Notes are numbered to correspond with quotes.

3. Trump's view of Putin is at odds with a majority of Americans including members of the Republican Party. Positive views

of Russia's invasion of Ukraine align more with dictators in Syria and Cuba.

8. **Crimea:** On March 18, 2014, masked Russian troops invaded Crimea and declared it a part of Russia. Trump made admiring and supportive comments about the incursion on April 28.

10. We have not been able to locate any records that suggest Putin met with or spoke with Trump during this time.

11. Trump praised Russian President Putin effusively during a Miss Universe pageant in Russia while negotiating with Russian President Putin to open a Trump Hotel in Moscow.

13. **Edward Snowden** was a former American counterintelligence agent who leaked massive amounts of highly classified information on U.S. espionage activities. Snowden was granted Russian citizenship on September 26, 2022, by Putin.

14. Trump frequently refers to himself in the 3rd person.

18. Trump compared the leadership of Obama and Putin after the latter had ordered the invasion of a sovereign country. Russia's aggression in Ukraine has been condemned as a violation of international law by the United Nations, the European Union, and the United States.

19. The "60 Minutes" episode consisted of two entirely unrelated segments. One focused on Trump and the other focused on Putin.

21. **Putin's leadership:** Trump said to "Morning Joe" host Joe Scarborough that Putin was a better leader than Obama and dismissed allegations that the Russian president "kills journalists that don't agree with him."

22. **Alexander Litvinenko** was a high-profile former Russian intelligence agent who was poisoned in the U.K. The consensus of most security agencies was that the manner and location of his assassination meant clearance would have allegedly come from the highest sources inside the Kremlin.

23. **Russia:** In August 2020 the U.S. Senate Intelligence Committee issued a report finding that the Trump presidential campaign chairman's interaction with Russian intelligence officials during the 2016 election posed a "grave counterintelligence threat."

24. We were unable to find any record or document where Putin refers to Trump as a genius.

26. NATO contributions are not paid to the United States, and there are no outstanding payments due.

30. **Emails:** It is during this news conference that Trump called on Russia to find U.S. Secretary of State Hillary Clinton's deleted emails.

32. **Russian President Vladimir Putin:** In response to a question on Fox if he had ever met Putin, he replied yes, directly contradicting previous statements that he had not.

33. According to an indictment from Special Counsel Robert Mueller, Russian officials began to target email addresses associated with Hillary Clinton's personal and campaign offices "on or around" the same day Trump called on Russia to find emails that he alleged were missing.

    As reported by PBS, July 13, 2018, After the July, 2016 news conference, critics slammed Trump for apparently encouraging foreign actors to steal information from his [political] opponent.

34. **Allies' payments:** In this interview with The New York Times, Trump suggests there are allies who are delinquent in meeting the 2% of GDP defense spending targets. The targets, however, are non-binding, leaving it to individual countries to fund defense as they can. There are no outstanding contributions from allies. Payments are not made to the U.S.

35. **Putin:** During a news conference, Trump was asked about his relationship with Putin.

36. **NATO and NAFTA:** The comment regarding NATO was made on June 28, the day before a G7 summit, for maximum impact. The reference to NAFTA (North American Free Trade Agreement) is a false equivalence. NATO is a voluntary alliance whereas NAFTA was a formal agreement between the U.S., Mexico, and Canada to promote free trade by preventing any one single government from passing legislation to secure its own industries. For more detail see: https://www.managementstudyguide.com/is-nafta-as-bad-as-donald-trump-says.htm

37. **NATO spending:** Between 2016 and 2019, spending by NATO allies increased by 15% (approximately $40 billion). Between 2014 and 2016, spending had increased by 4.8% or $12 billion, according to Factcheck.org.

39. **Trump-Putin meetings:** As of October 2019, Trump and Putin had five face-to-face encounters and 16 telephone calls.

40. **Putin's recognition** of Ukrainian breakaway regions as "independent" was viewed as a violation of international law and a major escalation of the conflict leading to Russia's invasion.

43. This Tweet appeared five days following the intense backlash to Trump's repeated admiring Tweets of Putin's invasion of Ukraine.

46. **NATO spending:** Spending increases by NATO allies pre-dated Trump's election in 2016. For more information: https://www.npr.org/2018/07/11/628137185/fact-check-trumps-claims-on-nato-spending

TRUMP ON HEALTH CARE

"Who knew health care could be so complicated."
February 27, 2017 National Governors Association

1. "Working out detailed plans will take time. But the goal should be clear: Our people are our greatest asset. We must take care of our own. We must have universal health care."

   2000 "The America We Deserve" by Donald Trump and Dave Shiflett

2. "We will repeal Obamacare and replace it with something terrific."

   2015 campaign trail via CNN

3. "Nobody knows health care better than Donald Trump."

   January 30, 2016, ABC's "This Week with George Stephanopoulos"

4. "Together we're going to deliver real change that once again puts Americans first. That begins with immediately repealing and replacing the disaster known as Obamacare. ... You're going to have such great health care, at a tiny fraction of the cost — and it's going to be so easy."

   October 2016 campaign rally in Florida

5. "ObamaCare is a total disaster. Hillary Clinton wants to save it by making it even more expensive. Doesn't work, I will REPEAL AND REPLACE!"

   November 2016 Tweet

6. "We have come up with a solution that's really, really I think very good."

   2017 governors meeting at the White House

7. "In a short period of time I understood everything there was to know about health care. And we did the right negotiating, and actually it's a very interesting subject."

   May 2017 Time magazine

8. "So pre-existing conditions are a tough deal, because you are basically saying from the moment the insurance, you're 21 years old, you start working and you're paying $12 a year for insurance, and by the time you're 70, you get a nice plan. Here's something where you walk up and say, 'I want my insurance.' It's a very tough deal, but it is something that we're doing a good job of."

   July 2017 The New York Times

9. "I know a lot about health care."

   July 2017 The New York Times

10. "We have a plan that I think is going to be fantastic. It's going to be released fairly soon, I think it's going to be something special ... I think you're going to like what you hear."

    2017 gathering of health insurance company CEOs

11. "My poll numbers are going through the roof. You know why? I really believe a big part of it is Obamacare, because we're going to repeal it and replace it. Obamacare has to be replaced. And we will do it and we will do it very, very quickly. It is a catastrophe. If we don't repeal and replace Obamacare, we will destroy American health care forever."

    2017 campaign speech video from MSNBC

12. "Obamacare is collapsing. It's dead. It's gone. There's nothing to compare anything to because we don't have health care in this country. You just look at what's happening. Aetna just

pulled out. Other insurance companies are pulling out. We don't have health care. Obamacare is a fallacy. It's gone."

May 2017 press conference at the White House

13. "We will unleash something that's gonna be terrific. And remember this, before Obamacare you had a lot of people that were very, very happy with their health care. And now those people in many cases don't even have health care. They don't even have anything that's acceptable to them. Remember this, keep your doctor, keep your plan, 100 percent."

    January 25, 2017, interview with ABC's David Muir

14. "...we are going to have a better plan, much better healthcare, much better service treatment, a plan where you can have access to the doctor that you want and the plan that you want. We're gonna have a much better health care plan at much less money."

    2017 Tweet

15. "And remember Obamacare is ready to explode. And you interviewed me a couple of years ago. I said '17 -- right now, this year, '17 is going to be a disaster.' I'm very good at this stuff. '17 is going to be a disaster cost-wise for Obamacare. It's going to explode in '17."

    January 2017 interview with ABC's David Muir

16. "ObamaCare is a broken mess. Piece by piece we will now begin the process of giving America the great HealthCare it deserves!"

    October 2017 Tweet

17. "ObamaCare is dead, and the Democrats are obstructionists, no ideas or votes, only obstruction. It is solely up to the 52 Republican Senators!"

    July 2017 Tweet

18. "Republicans will soon be known as the party of healthcare."
March 2019 speech

19. "Currently, there are insufficient funding sources designated for the federal government to use in response to a severe influenza pandemic."
October 2019 Trump administration

20. "We have it totally under control. It's one person coming in from China. It's going to be just fine."
January 28, 2020, Tweet

21. – 23. "We pretty much have it shut down coming in from China."
February 2, 2020

Responding to a National Security advisee calling the pandemic the biggest national security threat the Trump administration could face:
"I think the virus is going to be— it's going to be fine."
February 10, 2020

"Looks like by April, you know in theory when it gets a little warmer, it miraculously goes away."
February 2020

24. "We will have Healthcare which is FAR BETTER than ObamaCare, at a FAR LOWER COST - BIG PREMIUM REDUCTION. PEOPLE WITH PRE-EXISTING CONDITIONS WILL BE PROTECTED AT AN EVEN HIGHER LEVEL THAN NOW. HIGHLY UNPOPULAR AND UNFAIR INDIVIDUAL MANDATE ALREADY TERMINATED. YOU'RE WELCOME!"
October 2020 Tweet

25. " ... he (Chinese President Xi Jinping) will be successful, especially as the weather starts to warm & the virus hopefully becomes weaker, and then gone. Great discipline is taking

place in China, as President Xi strongly leads what will be a very successful operation. We are working closely with China to help!"

February 7, 2020, Tweet

26. "Coronavirus is very much under control in the USA … the Stock Market is starting to look very good to me!"

February 24, 2020

27. "CDC and my Administration are doing a GREAT job of handling Coronavirus."

February 5, 2020

28 – 29. "Because of all we've done, the risk to the American people remains very low. … When you have 15 people, and the 15 within a couple of days is going to be down to close to zero. That's a pretty good job we've done."

February 2020

"You may ask about the coronavirus, which is very well under control in our country. We have very few people with it, and the people that have it are … getting better. They're all getting better. … As far as what we're doing with the new virus, I think that we're doing a great job."

February 2020

30. Q: This is spreading — or is going to spread, maybe, within communities. That's the expectation.
Trump: It may. It may.
Q: Does that worry you?
Trump: No. … No, because we're ready for it. It is what it is. We're ready for it. We're really prepared. … We hope it doesn't spread. There's a chance that it won't spread too, and there's a chance that it will, and then it's a question of at what level.

February 2020 The Washington Post

31. "It's going to disappear. One day, it's like a miracle, it will disappear."

February 2020

32. ". … We only have 15 people, and they are getting better, and hopefully they're all better. There's one who is quite sick, but maybe he's gonna be fine. … We're prepared for the worst, but we think we're going to be very fortunate."

February 2020

33. "Now the Democrats are politicizing the coronavirus. … And this is their new hoax."

February 2020

34. "We did an interview on Fox last night, a town hall. I think it was very good. And I said: 'Calm. You have to be calm. It'll go away.'"

March 2020

35. "We're doing very well, and we've done a fantastic job."

March 2020

36. "And it hit the world. And we're prepared, and we're doing a great job with it. And it will go away. Just stay calm. It will go away."

March 2020

37. "FDA will bring, additionally, 1.4 million tests on board next week and 5 million within a month. I doubt we'll need anywhere near that."

March 2020

38. "It's going to go away. … The United States, because of what I did and what the administration did with China, we have 32 deaths at this point … when you look at the kind of numbers that you're seeing coming out of other countries, it's pretty amazing when you think of it."

March 2020

39. "This is a very contagious virus. It's incredible. But it's something that we have tremendous control over."

March 2020

40. "If you're talking about the virus, no, that's not under control for any place in the world. ... I was talking about what we're doing is under control, but I'm not talking about the virus."

March 2020

41. "America will again and soon be open for business. ... Parts of our country are very lightly affected."

March 2020

42. "It's hard not to be happy with the job we're doing, that I can tell you."

March 2020

43. "It's going to go away, hopefully at the end of the month and if not, it hopefully will be soon after that."

March 2020

44. "If we didn't do any testing, we would have very few cases."

May 2020

45. "Some wacko in China just released a statement blaming everybody other than China for the Virus which has now killed hundreds of thousands of people. Please explain to this dope that it was the 'incompetence of China', and nothing else, that did this mass Worldwide killing!"

May 2020 Tweet

46. "This is going to go away without a vaccine."

May 2020

47. "The numbers are very minuscule compared to what it was. It's dying out."

June 2020

48. "The Federal Reserve is wrong so often. I see the numbers also and do MUCH better than they do. We will have a very good Third Quarter, a great Fourth Quarter, and one of our best ever years in 2021. We will also soon have a Vaccine & Therapeutics/Cure. That's my opinion. WATCH!

June 2020 Tweet

49. "We have more Cases because we do more Testing."

July 2020

50. "Kung Flu. Not racist at all. It comes from China. I want to be accurate."

July 2020 Trump rally in Tulsa, Oklahoma

51. "If we tested less, there would be less cases."

August 2020

52. "It's going away, but we're also going to have vaccines very soon."

August 2020

53. "We're rounding the turn on the pandemic."

September 2020

54. "I think the vaccine is going to come very soon, very soon. And with it or without it, we're rounding the turn."

September 2020

55. "We are rounding the corner on covid. We're rounding it and rounding it rapidly, plus we have vaccines coming very soon and we have therapeutics which have already made a big dent, a tremendous dent."

September 2020

56. "We're doing great, we're rounding it with or without (a vaccine)."

September

57. "It affects virtually nobody. It's an amazing thing."

September 2020 campaign rally in Ohio

58. "The end of the pandemic is in sight."

October 2020

59. "Right now I'm fighting to eradicate the virus, and we're doing really a good job, we're rounding the turn."

October 2020

60. "Excess mortality, we're a winner on the excess mortality, and what we've done has been amazing and we have done an amazing job, and it's rounding the corner and we have the vaccines coming and we have the therapies coming."

October 2020

61. "The light at the end of the tunnel is near."

October 2020

62. "The pandemic, it's rounding the turn, vaccines are coming, and I look fine, don't I?"

October 2020

63. "Our vaccine will eradicate the virus. By the way, we have it, but whether we have it or not, it's rounding the turn. It's rounding the turn."

October 2020

64. "We'll quickly eradicate the virus and wipe out the China plague once and for all. And let me tell you, we are rounding the corner anyway, but we have the vaccines coming very shortly."

November 2020

65. "...Obamacare is a joke! Deductible is far too high and the overall cost is ridiculous. My Administration has gone out of its way to manage OC much better than previous, but it PEOPLE WITH PRE-EXISTING is still no good. I will

ALWAYS PROTECT CONDITIONS, ALWAYS, ALWAYS ALWAYS!!!"

June 2020 Tweet

66. "We're signing a health care plan within two weeks, a full and complete health care plan."

July 2020 Fox News

67. "I do want to say that we're going to be introducing a tremendous health care plan sometime prior -- hopefully, prior to the end of the month. It's just completed now."

August 2020 Press Briefing

68. "So we will be pursuing a major executive order, requiring health insurance companies to cover all pre-existing conditions for all of its customers."

August 2020 press briefing at Trump's Bedminster, New Jersey, Golf Club

69. "I am the healthiest president that ever lived."

August 7, 2022 CPAC in Dallas, Texas

70. "Something how Dr. Fauci is revered by the Lame Stream Media as such a great professional, having done, they say, such an incredible job, yet he works for me and the Trump Administration, and I am in no way given any credit for my work. Gee, could this just be more Fake News?"

January 2021 Tweet

71. "He was the White House doctor. He was a great doctor. He was an admiral, a Doctor, and now he's a congressman. I said, 'Which is the best if you had your choice?' and he sort of indicated doctor because he loved looking at my body. It was so strong and powerful."

August 7, 2022 CPAC in Dallas, Texas

NOTES

Notes are numbered to correspond with quotes.

1. As a candidate or as president, Trump never presented a healthcare plan to the American people or to Congress. Trump also failed to deliver on his promise to repeal or replace the Affordable Care Act also known as Obamacare.

5. By the 2016 election, 12.7 million Americans had enrolled in Obamacare. As of April 2022, over 35 million people have Obamacare coverage.

6. Trump made numerous promises to reveal an alternative health-care plan, but never presented an alternative plan to the American people or to Congress.

8. This widely published quote was never fully explained by Trump.

11. By 2016, 69% of Republicans wanted to repeal Obamacare. A post-election survey by Kaiser Family Foundation found only 1 in 4 Americans want Obamacare repealed.

13. A 2008 Commonwealth Fund poll found 82% of Americans wanted the health-care system overhauled.
Source: https://www.healthinsurance.org/blog/the-good-old-days-before-obamacare/#:~:text=82%25%20wanted%20the%20system%20overhauled,Fund%2C%20which%20commissioned%20the%20poll.

15. By April 2022, 35 million Americans had signed up for Obamacare.
Source: https://policyadvice.net/insurance/insights/affordable-care-act-statistics/#:~:text=According%20to%20this%20news%20article,care%20coverage%20through%20Obamacare%20Act.

19. The quote comes from a report about pandemic preparedness. The Obama administration established the

National Security Council global health unit for pandemics. On December 18, 2018, the Trump administration disbanded the White House pandemic response team.
Source: https://www.businessinsider.com/coronavirus-trump-admin-training-simulation-predicted-current-failures-2020-3

21.-23. As of December 31, 2022, the number of both confirmed and presumptive positive cases of the COVID-19 disease reported in the United States had reached 101 million with over one million deaths reported among these cases.

25. Chinese President Xi Jinping knew of the coronavirus by December 2019 but suppressed the information and forbade its discussion. Early global intervention likely could have saved thousands of lives.
Source: https://www.washingtonpost.com/opinions/global-opinions/what-did-xi-jinping-know-about-the-coronavirus-and-when-did-he-know-it/2020/02/19/35482fe2-5340-11ea-b119-4faabac6674f_story.html

Eight months after this comment, the U.S. had over 20 million infections and over 346,000 deaths.
Source: https://www.ajmc.com/view/a-timeline-of-covid19-developments-in-202

28. -29. Despite Trump's assurances, federal health officials added that they were preparing for a pandemic that would close schools and businesses. Eleven months later 95,245 people died from Covid-19 in one month alone, according to Johns Hopkins University.

31. **COVID statistics:** By November 2022, US recorded a total of 97.3 million cases and 1.07 million deaths

37. **COVID tests:** As of March 2020, the U.S. had performed a total of 472 tests.

41. **Mandates:** The U.S. lifted Covid 19 negative test requirements for international travel on June 12, 2022. As of November 2022, many states repealed mask mandates. The CDC has shortened quarantine recommendations to five days following a positive test.

48. **Real GDP** in 2020 decreased by 3.5% from 2019. Personal dollar income decreased by $541.5 billion in the third quarter and by $339.7 billion in the fourth quarter and disposable income decreased by 9.5%.
Source: https://www.bea.gov/news/2021/gross-domestic-product-4th-quarter-and-year-2020-advance-estimate

52. **COVID vaccines:** The FDA issued the first Emergency Use Authorization (EUA) of the Pfizer vaccine for people over age 16 on December 11, 2020. First deliveries began December 14, 2020.
The FDA issued the second EUA for the Moderna vaccine on December 18, 2020, and the third for the Janssen vaccine was issued on Feb 27, 2021. Formal FDA approval for the Pfizer vaccine was issued August 23, 2021. Approximately 10% of the population had received vaccines by spring 2021.

66. Never happened. See Note 1.

68. The passage of Obamacare in 2010 required insurance companies to cover pre-existing conditions making Trump's proposed executive order irrelevant.

69. **Trump's health:** Trump claims he is quoting Dr. Ronnie Jackson.

71. **White House physician:** Referring to Dr Ronnie Jackson.

PRESIDENTIAL THOUGHTS

Actually, throughout my life, my two greatest assets have been mental stability and being, like, really smart."
January 2018 On Travel to Camp David

1. "I would never buy Ivana any decent jewels or pictures. Why give her negotiable assets?"
   1990 Vanity Fair interview

2. "Black guys counting my money! I hate it. The only kind of people I want counting my money are short guys that wear yarmulkes every day. ... I think that the guy is lazy. And it's probably not his fault, because laziness is a trait in blacks. It really is, I believe that. It's not anything they can control."
   1991 Trumped! by John O'Donnell

3. "The stuff O'Donnell wrote about me is probably true."
   1997 Playboy interview

4. "To be blunt, people would vote for me. They just would. Why? Maybe because I'm so good looking."
   1999 The New York Times

5. "I'm intelligent. Some people would say I'm very, very, very intelligent."
   2000 Fortune Magazine interview

6. "I think Viagra is wonderful if you need it, if you have medical issues, if you've had surgery. I've just never needed it. Frankly, I wouldn't mind if there were an anti-Viagra, something with the opposite effect. I'm not bragging. I'm just lucky. I don't need it."
   2004 Playboy interview

7. "As a kid, I was making a building with blocks in our playroom. I didn't have enough. So, I asked my younger brother Robert

if I could borrow some of his. He said, 'Okay, but you have to give them back when you're done.' I used all of my blocks, then all of his blocks, and when I was done, I had a great building, which I then glued together. Robert never did get those blocks back."

2004 Esquire magazine

8. "My favorite part (of "*Pulp Fiction"*]) is when Sam has his gun out in the diner and he tells the guy to tell his girlfriend to shut up. 'Tell that bitch to be cool. Say: Bitch be cool.' I love those lines."

   2005 "Trump Nation – The Art of Being The Donald" by Timothy L. O'Brien

9. "She does have a very nice figure ... if (Ivanka) weren't my daughter, perhaps I'd be dating her.

   2006 appearance on "The View"

10. "The beauty of me is that I'm very rich."

    2011, 2016, 2018 repeated quote and tweet

11. "I have a great relationship with the blacks."

    April 2011 Talk 1300

12. "My fingers are long and beautiful, as, it has been well documented, are various other parts of my body."

    2011 New York Post

13. "I look very much forward to showing my financials, because they are huge."

    April 2011 Time magazine

14. "We build a school, we build a road, they blow up the school, we build another school, we build another road, they blow them up, we build again. In the meantime, we can't get a fucking school in Brooklyn."

    April 2011 speech in Las Vegas
    (On foreign aid)

15. "I have never seen a thin person drinking Diet Coke."

2012 Tweet

16. "Who wouldn't take Kate's (Middleton) picture and make lots of money if she does the nude sunbathing thing. Come on Kate!"

September 2012 Tweet

17. "The concept of global warming was created by and for the Chinese in order to make US manufacturing non-competitive."

November 2012 Tweet

18. "Sorry losers and haters, but my I.Q. is one of the highest – and you all know it! Please don't feel so stupid or insecure, it's not your fault."

May 2013 Tweet

19. "26,000 unreported sexual assaults in the military — only 238 convictions. What did these geniuses expect when they put men & women together?"

May 2013 Tweet

20. "How amazing, the State Health Director who verified copies of Obama's 'birth certificate' died in plane crash today. All others lived."

December 2013 Tweet

21. "Obama's wind turbines kill 13-39 million birds and bats every year!"

May 2014 Tweet

22. "I know words, I have the best words."

December2015 campaign rally in South Carolina

23. "We're rounding 'em up in a very humane way, in a very nice way. And they're going to be happy because they want to

be legalized. And, by the way, I know it doesn't sound nice. But not everything is nice."

2015 "60 Minutes" interview
(On immigration)

24. "The line of 'Make America great again,' the phrase, that was mine, I came up with it about a year ago, and I kept using it, and everybody's using it, they are all loving it. I don't know, I guess I should copyright it, maybe I have copyrighted it."

2015 March Rolling Stone magazine

25. "I will build a great, great wall on our southern border. And I will have Mexico pay for that wall."

June 2015 Tweet and at numerous campaign rallies

26. "I could stand in the middle of Fifth Avenue and shoot somebody and I wouldn't lose any voters."

2015 campaign rally in Sioux Center, Iowa

27. "I think I could have stopped it because I have very tough illegal immigration policies, and people aren't coming into this country unless they're vetted and vetted properly."

October 2015 Fox News Hannity

28. "I'm the most successful person ever to run for the presidency, by far. Nobody's ever been more successful than me. I'm the most successful person ever to run. Ross Perot isn't successful like me. Romney – I have a Gucci store that's worth more than Romney."

June2015 Des Moines Register

29. "If Hillary Clinton can't satisfy her husband what makes her think she can satisfy America?"

April 2015 Tweet

30. "John McCain is not a war hero. He's a war hero – he's a war hero 'cause he was captured. I like people that weren't captured, OK, I hate to tell you."

2015 Iowa Family Leadership Summit

31. "Why can't we use nuclear weapons?"

August 2016 recorded during meeting with foreign policy advisers

32. "Happy New Year to all, including to my many enemies and those who have fought me and lost so badly they just don't know what to do. Love!"

December 2016 Tweet

33. "Why would Kim Jong-un insult me by calling me old, when I would never call him short and fat? Oh well, I try so hard to be his friend and maybe someday that will happen."

November 2017 Tweet

34. "We condemn in the strongest possible terms this egregious display of hatred, bigotry, and violence on many sides. On many sides."

August 2017 The Washington Post

35. "Sorry, losers and haters. My IQ is one of the highest and you all know it. Please don't feel so stupid or insecure, it's not your fault."

October 2017 Tweet

36. "It's freezing and snowing in New York – we need global warming!"

December 29, 2017, Tweet

37. "Despite the constant negative press covfefe."

May 31, 2017, Tweet

(Unknown what Trump was referring to)

38. “Actually, throughout my life, my two greatest assets have been mental stability and being, like, really smart.”

January 2018 Camp David trip
(repeated on various occasions)

39. “Why are we having all these people from shithole countries coming here?”

2018 White House meeting

40. “Kim Jung-un speaks and his people sit up at attention. I want my people to do the same.”

June 2018 “Fox & Friends”

41. “He’s now president for life. President for life! No, he’s great. And look, he was able to do that. I think it’s great. Maybe we’ll have to give that a shot someday.”

Recorded March 2018 closed-door meeting

42. “I went from VERY successful businessman, to top TV Star … to President of the United States (on my first try). I think that would qualify as not smart, but genius … and a very stable genius at that!”

January 6, 2018, Tweet

43. “I wouldn’t say I’m a feminist. I think that would be, maybe, going too far.”

January 2018 Piers Morgan interview

44. “So many people at the higher ends of intelligence loved my press conference performance in Helsinki. Putin and I discussed many important subjects at our earlier meeting. We got along well which truly bothered many haters who wanted to see a boxing match. Big results will come!”

July 2018 Tweet

45. “North Korean Leader Kim Jong Un just stated that the “Nuclear Button is on his desk at all times.” Will someone from his depleted and food starved regime please inform

him that I too have a Nuclear Button, but it is a much bigger & more powerful one than his, and my Button works!"

January 2018 Tweet

46. "Crazy Joe Biden is trying to act like a tough guy. Actually, he is weak, both mentally and physically, and yet he threatens me, for the second time, with physical assault. He doesn't know me, but he would go down fast and hard, crying all the way."

March 2018 Tweet

47. "Mike Pompeo, Director of the CIA, will become our new Secretary of State. He will do a fantastic job! Thank you to Rex Tillerson for his service! Gina Haspel will become the new Director of the CIA, and the first woman so chosen. Congratulations to all."

March 2018 Tweet

48. "I called President Putin of Russia to congratulate him on his election victory (in past, Obama called him also). The Fake News Media is crazed because they wanted me to excoriate him. They are wrong! Getting along with Russia (and others) is a good thing, not a bad thing … …"

March 2018 Tweet

49. "NEVER, EVER THREATEN THE UNITED STATES AGAIN OR YOU WILL SUFFER CONSEQUENCES THE LIKES OF WHICH FEW THROUGHOUT HISTORY HAVE EVER SUFFERED BEFORE. WE ARE NO LONGER A COUNTRY THAT WILL STAND FOR YOUR DEMENTED WORDS OF VIOLENCE & DEATH. BE CAUTIOUS!"

July 23, 2018, Tweet

50. "I had a GREAT meeting with Putin and the Fake News used every bit of their energy to try and disparage it. So bad for our country!"

July 2018 Tweet

51. "Our army manned the air, it rammed the ramparts, it took over the airports, it did everything it had to do, and at Fort McHenry, under the rockets' red glare, it had nothing but victory."

July 4, 2019, speech
(Praising efforts of the American Revolutionary War in the 1770s)

52. "I had a meeting at the Pentagon with lots of generals ... they were like from a movie, better looking than Tom Cruise and stronger. And I had more generals than I've ever seen."

2019 Cabinet Meeting

53. "There are those that say they have never seen the queen have a better time, a more animated time."

2019 state visit to the United Kingdom

54. "When during the campaign I would say, 'Mexico is going to pay for the wall', obviously I never said this and I never meant they're going to write out a check."

January 2019 Tweet

55. "I think Pocahontas, she's finished, she's out. She's gone. No, when it was found that I had more Indian blood in me than she did."

2019 campaign rally in Wisconsin

56. "Rex Tillerson, a man who is 'dumb as a rock' and totally ill prepared and ill equipped to be Secretary of State, made up a story (he got fired) that I was out prepared by Vladimir Putin at a meeting in Hamburg, Germany. I don't think Putin would agree. Look how the U.S. is doing!"

May 2019 Tweet

57. "Very good call yesterday with President Putin of Russia. Tremendous potential for a good/great relationship with Russia, despite what you read and see in the Fake News

Media. Look how they have misled you on 'Russia Collusion.' The World can be a better and safer place. Nice!"

May 2019 Tweet

58. "So interesting to see 'Progressive' Democrat Congresswomen, who originally came from countries whose governments are a complete and total catastrophe, the worst, most corrupt and inept anywhere in the world (if they even have a functioning government at all), now loudly ... and viciously telling the people of the United States, the greatest and most powerful Nation on earth, how our government is to be run. Why don't they go back and help fix the totally broken and crime infested places from which they came. Then come back and show us how ... it is done. These places need your help badly, you can't leave fast enough. I'm sure that Nancy Pelosi would be very happy to quickly work out free travel arrangements!"

July 2019 Tweet

59. "I tested positively toward negative, right? So, no. I tested perfectly this morning, meaning I tested negative. But that's a way of saying it. Positively toward the negative."

May 2020 to reporters outside the White House

60. "I'm an environmentalist. A lot of people don't understand that. I think I know more about the environment than most people."

October 2020 Tweet

61. "Covid, Covid, Covid is the unified chant of the Fake News Lamestream Media. They will talk about nothing else until November 4th., when the Election will be (hopefully!) over. Then the talk will be in how low the death rate is, plenty of hospital rooms, & many tests of young people."

October 2020 Tweet

62. “Tonight, @FLOTUS and I tested positive for COVID-19. We will begin our quarantine and recovery process immediately. We will get through this TOGETHER!”

October 2020 Tweet

63. “Not my Wall, which will soon be finished (and Mexico will pay for the Wall!). Totally unrelated, but I think Steve will be just fine. By the way, is this the same job hopping Tim O’Brien that headed Mini Mike Bloomberg’s humiliating 2 Billion Dollar Presidential run? Debate prep!”

October 2020 Tweet

64. “STOP THE COUNT”

November 2020 election night Tweet
(On realizing defeat was imminent)

65. “We have it totally under control. It’s one person coming in from China. It’s going to be just fine.”

January 2020 Tweet

66. “Nobody’s ever been treated badly like me ... Although they do say Abraham Lincoln was treated really badly.”

February 2020 Tweet

67. “I see disinfectant, where it knocks it out in a minute, one minute, and is there a way we can do something like that by injection inside, or almost a cleaning. Because you see it gets in the lungs and it does a tremendous number on the lungs, it’d be interesting to check that. So, you’re going to have to use medical doctors, but it sounds interesting to me. So, we’ll see. But the whole concept of the light, the way it kills it in one minute, that’s pretty powerful.”

April 2020 at press briefing with William Bryan, head of Science and Technology, Department of Homeland Security, and Dr. Deborah Birx, White House coronavirus response coordinator

68. "For the 1/100th (sic) time, the reason we show so many cases, compared to other countries that haven't done nearly as well as we have, is that our TESTING is much bigger and better."

November 2020 Tweet

69. "Many people say that it is Patriotic to wear a face mask when you can't socially distance. There is nobody more Patriotic than me, your favorite President!"

July 2020 Tweet

70. "We believe these people are thieves. The big city machines are corrupt. This was a stolen election. Best pollster in Britain wrote this morning that this clearly was a stolen election, that it's impossible to imagine that Biden outran Obama in some of these states."

November 2020 Tweet
(On election results)

71. "...Most corrupt election in history, by far. We won!!!"

December 2020 Tweet

72. "Look at this man, he's the King of Europe!"

January 2021

73. "These are the things and events that happen when a sacred landslide election victory is so unceremoniously & viciously stripped away from great patriots who have been badly & unfairly treated for so long. Go home with love & in peace. Remember this day forever."

January 2021

NOTES

Notes are numbered to correspond with quotes.

1. **Ivana Trump** was Donald Trump's first wife. They had three children together: Donald Jr., Ivanka and Eric Trump. Born

in Czechoslovakia (now known as the Czech Republic) in 1949, she was a businesswoman, socialite, model and author. She died in July 2022.

3. **John O'Donnell** is the former president of Trump Plaza Hotel and Casino in Atlantic City. He wrote a book titled "Trumped!: The Inside Story of the Real Donald Trump — His Cunning Rise and Spectacular Fall."

5. **IQ:** Trump has never revealed his IQ score or his SAT scores. He directed his "fixer" and attorney Michael Cohen to threaten former high school, colleges, and the College Board never to release his grades or SAT scores.

9. "**The View"** is a daytime panel TV show hosted exclusively by women who discuss popular topics of the day.

11. **Racial incidents:** There is a long list of racially based incidents and comments associated with Trump and the Trump business. Probably the first on record is the Department of Justice suit against the Trump organization for discrimination against black tenants in 1973. Trump has made well-documented racially charged comments, from not wanting black accountants to the Obama birth certificate conspiracy theory and other generalizations, offensive to many.
Source: https://www.vox.com/2016/7/25/12270880/donald-trump-racist-racism-history

13. **Tax records:** Trump has consistently refused to release his tax records or any other financial information and fought in courts to keep any financial information secret.

21. **Bird deaths:** Three major studies in the US (2022) estimate bird deaths at a rate of between 100,000 to 450,000 a year. Birds are killed by collisions with buildings at 1 billion per year in the U.S. cats kill around 1 to 4 billion birds in the U.S. per year.

22. **Vocabulary:** Analysis of Trump's first 30,000 words uttered as president found he speaks at a third grade to seventh grade reading level. Mr. Trump's vocabulary and grammatical structure is "significantly more simple, and less diverse" than any president since Herbert Hoover.
    Source: https://www.independent.co.uk/news/world/americas/us-politics/trump-language-level-speaking-skills-age-eight-year-old-vocabulary-analysis-a8149926.html?r=76164

24. **MAGA:** The slogan "Make America Great Again" was Ronald Reagan's 1980 campaign slogan with George H.W. Bush. Bill Clinton also used it in his 1991 campaign announcement speech. Trump trademarked it in 2015 as a campaign slogan and then claimed it was his idea.

27. **9/11:** Trump suggests he would have stopped the 9/11 attack on the World Trade Center due to his strict immigration policies.

34. **Charlotteville,** Virginia was the location of a "Unite the Right" rally of white nationalists on August 11, 2017. The protest ostensibly was against the removal of a statue of Robert E. Lee. Clashes erupted between white nationalists and counter-protesters when a white nationalist drove his car into the crowd of opposing protesters, killing one person and injuring dozens of others.

41. **Xi Jinping:** CNN recording of meeting about Xi Jinping of China declaring himself president for life.

46. **Physical altercation with Joe Biden:** In March 2018, Biden suggested he "would have beat the Hell out of Trump in High School" for disrespecting women. He made a similar claim in 2016 when the infamous "Access Hollywood' tape came out.

47. **Rex Tillerson:** This Tweet essentially informed Rex Tillerson that he was fired. No previous communication

about this had taken place, and it represents arguably the first public firing by Tweet. Rex Tillerson is an American engineer and energy executive appointed by Trump as the 69th U.S. Secretary of State. Previously, he served as the Chairman and Chief Executive Officer of ExxonMobil from 2006-2016.

49. **Iran warning:** This Tweet to Iranian President Rouhani was entirely written in uppercase, and was in response to Rouhani criticizing Trump and stating that peace with Iran is "the mother of all peace, and war with Iran would be the mother of all wars."

50. **Meeting Putin:** Trump met with Russian President Vladimir Putin on July 16, 2018, in Helsinki. The summit was notable for Trump's public and shocking acceptance of Putin's denial of interference in the 2016 election despite advice of intelligence agencies.

51. **History:** The reference to taking over the airports during the Revolutionary War raised a number of eyebrows, particularly historians.

53. **The UK state visit** began with a barrage of vitriolic tweets as Marine 1 was landing at Buckingham Palace notably against London Mayor Sadiq Khan, whom Trump called a "stone cold loser."

54. **Mexico wall:** Trump has said Mexico will pay for the wall at least 20 times since 2015. Source: Fortune

55. **Pocahontas** is the nickname Trump gave Elizabeth Warren following her claim that she had Native American ancestry.

57. **Russian collusion** refers to the alleged collusion between Trump and his inner circle and the Russian government to secure the 2016 election.

58. **The Squad:** Of the four progressive congresswomen of color known as "the Squad" whom Trump told to go back home: Alexandria Ocasio-Cortez was born in the Bronx in New York City, Rashida Tlaib was born in Detroit, and Anna Pressley was born in Cincinnati. Ilhan Omar is a Somali American, who became an American citizen in 2000.

61. Two years into the pandemic, the coronavirus has killed Americans at far higher rates than people in other wealthy nations.

62. After downplaying the severity of the virus, President Trump received experimental antibodies and a steroid reserved for very ill patients to aid in his recovery. These treatments were not available to the public at that time.

64. Early returns on Election Night favored GOP voters, as expected, leading Trump to demand the count be stopped so as to exclude results from Democratic mail-in ballots.

65. **COVID-19:** As of December 31, 2022, the number of both confirmed and presumptive positive cases of the COVID-19 disease reported in the United States had reached 101 million with over one million deaths reported among these cases.

72. **Nigel Farage:** This Tweet refers to Nigel Farage, former leader of the UK Independence Party and then leader of the Brexit Party. Farage is one of the defining voices of the UK Brexit movement and while considered divisive by many, his influence on the Brexit narrative is undeniable.

73. **Storming the Capitol:** Trump's response to the storming of the U.S. Capitol on January 6, 2021.

Printed in the United States
by Baker & Taylor Publisher Services